The New Selling Model:

Targeting an Unsellable Generation

By

Richard C. Freeman

Disclaimer

Copyright © by. Richard C. Freeman 2023.All rights reserved.

Table of content

Introduction

Nowadays, a sales representative's ability to clinch a transaction depends more on the potential customer than it does on their skills. The availability of technology has made consumers more knowledgeable than ever.

Before making a choice, they may do research about the business, the goods, and even the salespeople. They are knowledgeable about what will work for them, can compare your proposal to all of your rivals, and will not be persuaded by a cold call.

How can you use this dynamic to close more deals? Most consumers make their financial decisions before ever speaking with a sales representative.

Most likely, before contacting you, your prospect has already selected two or three providers from their list. Successful salespeople are beginning to abandon the old hard-sell techniques as inbound marketing develops and take on the position of "trusted advisor."

Sales professionals need to communicate with clients on their chosen channels to stay on top of changing consumer emotions, which are now greatly affected by technology. Additionally, they must be genuine and supportive in both their messaging and strategy.

Every sales professional wants to conclude their month on a positive note, celebrating their victories, therefore organizations need to take these shifting attitudes into account. But regrettably, for the majority of sales representatives, it ends in despair over unmet goals. Problems that impact sales representatives' performance are frequently present. The problem is that sales representatives continue to sell despite these obstacles, which causes them to experience the same poor sales results each month.

Chapter 1

Typical sales problems and their solutions

Even the finest sales performers face obstacles in their careers. But rather than ignoring the problems with sales, they deal with them. Here are the most typical problems that sales representatives encounter and how to solve them.

1. One of the sales challenges is competing with rivals. Companies and Businesses are doing all it takes to outperform their rivals in the market, which has become a war zone. Competitors are experimenting with a variety of techniques to draw customers, from cutting rates to providing freebies. Such points are chosen by prospective customers and used as a defense to obtain the goods at a lower cost. The majority of the time, sales representatives are exposed to phrases like "The [X competitor] is offering a product at a much lower price" or "The [Y competitor] is offering a 4-month free subscription to their service." When faced with such situations or when they make an impetuous choice that hurts their sales, the majority of sales representatives freeze up. Solutions:

1. After conducting a thorough competitive study, list the rivals' strengths and flaws.

2. Determine how you are superior to your rivals and convey this to prospective customers. 3. Present case studies and reviews of pleased clients who choose you over your rivals.

2. Lack of time to sell is the second sales obstacle.

The to-do list for sales reps is extensive. A sales representative has several tasks to complete in a day, including gathering information about potential customers, writing sales emails, and updating data. Additionally, if things aren't ordered, looking for information takes longer. Sales representatives don't have enough time to concentrate on selling and strategy.

1. Automate the majority of your duties using an automation solution.

2. Make use of solutions that offer profile enrichment features to automatically retrieve important data about your prospects.

3. Instead of crafting each email from scratch, create and reuse email templates.

4. Use sales reports to keep track of your sales activity, and list your weekly responsibilities in order of importance.

5. As an alternative to using notebooks and notes, choose one platform to manage all of your customer data.

3. Third sales challenge: The prospect isn't responding. Most of the prospects quit replying after the first few exchanges. This quiet demotivates several sales representatives. They stop concentrating on the lead and go to another candidate. As a result, the majority of leads are not converted.

Solution:

1. Always follow up and never give up. To automate the follow-up, you can utilize software that enables you to build email and text sequences.

2. To enhance your response rate, use intriguing email subject lines and content.

3. Make an effort to contact another employee at the prospect's organization.

4. Make contact with the prospect at various times. Find the ideal moment to contact the prospect via phone or email.

5. Connect with your prospects using channels beyond than calls and emails, such as text messaging and social media.

4. Prospects' resistance throughout the negotiation is the fourth sales hurdle. In the sales process, the negotiating stage is when most transactions are lost. Many potential customers are hesitant to make concessions or establish common ground. Furthermore, the resistance of the prospect's irritates the sales representatives, who end up unpleasantly letting their frustration out.

Solution:

1. Remain composed throughout the negotiation, and consider your response before addressing a client's concern.

2. Research various bargaining strategies to cope with hesitant customers.

3. Identify the pressure points of the prospects and help them understand the effects of delaying action.

4. Start with a high price. Then present a cheap price with few features. Make the genuine pitch while the prospect is deciding between two offers.

5. Inability to manage criticism or rejection is the fifth sales hurdle. Most salespeople are unable to hear "NO" or take criticism well. They become discouraged. This event has an impact on their subsequent transaction since they are unable to concentrate due to their unhappiness about the rejection or criticism they received. Solution:

1. Get ready and practice a solid reply for when you receive a rejection.

2. Develop your EQ (Emotional Intelligence) abilities to prevent emotional hijacking.

3. Request a sample call session from your senior to get ready to manage rejection on sales calls.

4. Create several possibilities for yourself so that a small number of rejections won't have an impact on your goal.

6. Sixth sales challenge: sales education.

Most businesses have high standards but fail to provide their salespeople with the necessary training to deal with today's sophisticated customers. Low sales productivity is mostly caused by a lack of training. The majority of salespeople struggle to reach their sales objectives.

The first step in the solution is:

1. to identify the areas where training is necessary and ask management to fund it.

2. Watch live webinars to learn from professionals in the field.

3. Request frequent performance comments from the elders.

7. Failure to track deals is sales problem number seven. Numerous agreements might be in the sales pipeline. But regrettably, the majority of them become stuck for a lengthy time at some point in the selling pipeline and eventually fall through the breach. Many sales representatives miss out on chances because they lack insight into their sales pipeline.

The best CRM should be put into use as a solution.

1. You will have full insight into every stage of the sales process thanks to it.

2. Permit you to categorize and rank high-value trades so you can follow their development.

3. Keep you informed of all deal-related activities.

8. Lack of time to prospect is the eighth sales obstacle. A crucial part of the sales process is prospecting. However, most sales representatives find it difficult to set out a time for prospecting. Regularly making cold calls might introduce you to many potential chances. Therefore, do not neglect this crucial sales activity.

Solution:

1. Allocate a certain amount of time each day for cold calling.

2. Use a power dialer to speed up communication and save time.

3. Don't disregard making cold calls for any other activity.

9. 9th sales challenge: Unable to respond to prospects' inquiries Modern buyers are very smart and well-informed. They are updated with the current industry trends and popular technology. As a result, they frequently ask inquiries. The majority of the time, sales representatives are unable to respond to these inquiries. Do you also have this problem? If so, you must do the following actions.

Solution:

1. First of all, ensure you have good product knowledge.

2. list the questions that you often get and prepare for it.

3. Have a call with your senior.

Chapter 2

Myths and Reality of Sales

These fallacies have the potential to lower sales and lose top achievers. Research has been conducted over the past four decades to determine what distinguishes the world's top-performing sales representatives from their more typical competitors. We have spoken with more than a million customers, 25,000 sales managers, and more than 250,000 salespeople as part of that effort.

The term "the world's best" refers to salespeople who regularly rank in the top 25%, and frequently in the top 10%, of their organizations' sales teams. The absolute greatest performers typically sell four to ten times as much as average performers, according to our research. They provide considerably higher profitability. They tend to work for their respective businesses longer and form more enduring bonds with their clients.

As we investigated the essential elements associated with long-term business success, the last point—customer loyalty—became even more crucial. It turns out that customer loyalty is a considerably better indicator of business development than customer happiness. satisfied consumers will likely move elsewhere, but devoted consumers frequently remain. The sales force is therefore a crucial component in creating client loyalty, which is increasingly seen as the most crucial basis for ongoing corporate success.

According to additional Gallup research, the sales force (and other people with direct customer contact) is by far the most crucial factor in generating customer loyalty. While delivering a quality product or service is important, the sales force generates four times more customer loyalty than the product or service itself, and twice as much customer loyalty as advertising and marketing programs

Customer loyalty is, to put it simply, the most important factor in creating long-term business development. Customer loyalty is largely influenced by the sales force, and top sales producers account for the majority of this contribution.

Naturally, we were interested in finding out what made these top-performing salespeople unique. In-depth examinations of 170 companies' sales forces across 21 different industries were part of our research. After several interviews, a compelling picture emerged. the conclusions suprise us. The research challenges several generally held ideas about strong sales performance. We identified so many misunderstandings and falsehoods about sales that we thought of them collectively as the "big lie." the lowest quartiles. While the salespeople in the top quartile produced outstanding outcomes, those in the bottom quartile regularly lost clients and even lost customers.

We discovered that even in the greatest organizations, roughly 35% of the sales staff lacked the threshold skills required to perform consistently. As a result, this group consistently performs in the lower half of the distribution. However, many corporate rules are created to control weak producers rather than to reward exceptional workers. These regulations seldom aid underachievers in improving their performance; instead, they frequently obstruct excellent work and, in some cases, even drive away the most talented creators. Just consider the impact on client loyalty!

Selling organizations have no incentive to spread false information. Why then do the myths continue? Because the reality is concealed inside these falsehoods. Every misunderstanding has just enough truth in it to be rationally plausible.

For instance, we all have acquaintances who are fiercely competitive and effective salespeople. We may thus conclude that all successful salesmen are aggressive, as many businesses have done. This conclusion appears reasonable, but when we examine the evidence, we discover that it is just untrue. True, some successful salespeople are aggressive. Some people are not at all competitive. Also, some fiercely competitive individuals make terrible salespeople. They are worthless at selling. Being competitive is not sufficient to qualify someone as a great salesperson.

However, this is how myths are spread. We start with some genuine knowledge, generalize it, and get to an incorrect conclusion. It quickly gains acceptance as a given.

Our statistics disproved a lengthy array of presumptions regarding excellent sales success. Although false, misconceptions regarding education, training, connections, money, desire, or the best sales strategy have survived and served as the foundation for many firms' hiring criteria and management practices. We shall dispel each of these beliefs in the subsequent columns and contrast them with our discoveries. We'll also go through the actual distinctions between top salespeople and their competitors that we discovered.

We cannot overstate the significance of this knowledge given that businesses are faced with the task of delivering increasing revenue growth year after year. Increasing client loyalty is the secret to sustainable growth. A relatively small portion of your sales staff has a direct impact on customer loyalty. The secrets to creating a world-class selling organization are comprehending what makes them unique, utilizing this knowledge to attract additional individuals who are similar to them, and realizing how a manager inspires these star performers.

Chapter 3

Focusing the customer

What is customer focus and why is it crucial?

Businesses that put their customers first create an organizational culture devoted to raising customer satisfaction and establishing enduring connections with them. Good customer service, hearing (and acting upon) client input, and creating individualized customer experiences are a few examples of customer attention.

"Customer focus is the lens by which you analyze all your interactions with your customers." It's fundamental to your vision for your business and how you want your clients to see you.

Customer attention is vital for the following reasons,

1. Customers have high expectations: Following the crisis last year, more than 60% of consumers say

they now have higher expectations for customer service.

2. When firms offer their preferred method of contacting customer support, 93 percent of customers will spend more with them, and 90 percent will spend more with businesses that customize the customer service they provide.

3. Churn can result from a lack of customer attention; 61% of consumers say they would move to a company's competition after just one negative customer service encounter, and 76% say they would do so after several negative interactions.

4. If a business is customer-focused, customers are more likely to forgive mistakes made by that business: 74% of customers believe they will forgive a business for mistakes made after getting exceptional service.

5. Customer attention promotes loyalty and retention: Quality customer service increases client retention, according to 60% of corporate executives.

Four instances of client centricity

Being a customer-focused firm takes time, even after developing a successful customer focus strategy. To get anything done properly, you need to practice and make adjustments over time. From four organizations that achieved it, here are a few examples of how to run a customer-focused business.

1. first Zappos

Zappos unites the company via customer-centric ideals to demonstrate how the customer experience counts throughout the whole company. For instance, every worker answers customer service calls for the first two weeks of their employment.

2. The Four Seasons

With its white-glove customer service, which is built on forming genuine, personal connections with clients, The Four Seasons revolutionized luxury. As they would with a friend, visitors may contact the hotel through Twitter, Facebook Messenger, or SMS to make spa reservations, seek restaurant suggestions, or take advantage of special offers.

3. Postmates

To guarantee that customer input drives important product choices, Postmates' CX team collaborates with their product team and analytics team. As a result, observable gains are generated, such as a decrease in customer cancellations due to product changes.

4. Birchbox

Birchbox employs service recovery to identify consumer grievances before improving the situation to mend the connection.

How can you create a culture that is customer-focused?

You must first make sure you comprehend your consumers and their demands to create a customer-focused culture. Creating a single,

360-degree perspective of your customers from disparate, disconnected sources and, of course, being able to use that data to improve experiences are required for this.

1. You locate the best answer for them.

fostering empathy for customers. To get a fresh perspective on parts of your business you're not familiar with, try putting yourself in your consumers' shoes. For instance, you could think emphasizing a product's cutting-edge features will help a salesperson close a sale. However, people may be more eager to hear how it will make their lives simpler.

Improved customer attention should be a company-wide objective even if sales and customer service professionals are the front line in engaging with consumers.

Only 51% of consumers feel that businesses typically understand their requirements and expectations, despite 73% of customers believing that they do.

Provide non-customer-facing employees with the chance to interact with consumers or handle service calls, starting with the CEO, to gain firsthand knowledge of their needs. To obtain insight, collect and evaluate data, such as web analytics, attrition rates, and product use patterns. Then, ask consumers for comments.

You may learn a lot about your consumers' true opinions of your company by conducting surveys. Or create a customer advisory group that will meet multiple times a year to go through corporate goals, industry trends, and strategy. Customers' feedback findings should be distributed across your company.

Monitoring online conversations about your company through social listening is another effective strategy for cultivating a client-centered mentality. Try these social listening methods and keep an eye out for specific mentions of your business or products on Facebook, Twitter, Instagram, and other social media platforms.

a. Search for hashtags and direct mentions of your company, brand, or items. Keep in mind frequent misspellings. Although you know how to spell the name of your business or product, clients might not.

b. Keep track of the hashtags that your clients use. Your clients might not talk about your business or sector in the same words that you do. Follow people that have influential opinions in the industry or businesses that cater to your desired clientele. Follow the hashtags they employ.

C. Monitor the activities of rivals. Do you know what your competitors' customers are asking? Consider whether you should address the same queries in your own blog or marketing material if they keep coming up.

d. Request input from your audience. Do you have a special question? Instagram, Twitter, and Facebook all include polling features. Alternatively, just pose open-ended queries to your audience.

2. Create room for ideas

In response to their actions and behaviors, 62% of customers now expect businesses to adapt, according to the "State of the Connected Customer" study. Among Millennials and Generation Z, this rises to 67%.

While brilliant ideas may originate from anybody, many firms have typically reserved innovative concepts for a small number of individuals. Indeed, through co-creation platforms and programs, businesses like Unilever, Ikea, and Lego today actively include customers in problem-solving and the development of new products.

According to organizational expert Simon Sinek, a leader's job is not to generate all the brilliant ideas. A leader's job is to foster an environment where brilliant ideas may flourish.

3. Remove internal obstacles

bubbles, swim lanes, and silos. Even if organizational specialists may use various terminology, the fundamental issue is the same: Customers sense a disconnect when engaging with your company because client data is spread across many platforms held by various departments.

Although 78% of consumers say they anticipate constant department-to-department contacts, their expectations are not being met: 59% of respondents stated they frequently feel as though they are speaking with many departments rather than a single, cohesive corporation. The majority of consumers (66%) claimed that they frequently had to repeat or re-explain information to several agents. The creation of the more meaningful, individualized experiences that customers now expect from organizations is significantly hampered by disjointed data.

Silo dismantling is easier said than done. Businesses must strive to provide a comprehensive 360-degree customer view, nevertheless, to be customer-focused. They will be able to provide unified cross-channel client interaction by doing this.

4. Secure your data

The threshold for business is raised by innovations like artificial intelligence (AI) and the Internet of Things (IoT). Businesses are under pressure to advance since many consumers and corporate purchasers are willing to pay more for distinctive, first-to-market goods and services.

Customers want businesses to adopt new technology to improve customer experiences, according to 75% of them. The same percentage (74%) anticipates businesses to leverage current technology in novel ways to improve user experiences.

History has repeatedly demonstrated that it is better to cause trouble for yourself than to stand by and let someone else do it to you.

This can entail creating tailored suggestions based on a customer's browsing and purchase history. Alternatively, you might offer a consumer a discount on items they've explored by sending push alerts to their phone. Using chatbots to gather and validate information might also mean giving operators more time to focus on resolving consumer issues.

5. Designate a customer-focused ally

In the day-to-day operations of, well, running a business, the emphasis on the customer can be forgotten. A chief customer officer (CCO) is an excellent concept because of this.

The CCO's responsibility is to represent the interests of the customer and make sure that the business as a whole keeps the consumer in mind. They advocate for customers' demands, assist in directing the creation of goods and procedures, and pinpoint areas where teams' customer focus abilities need to be strengthened using data and research.

Additionally, they guarantee that having a strong customer focus brings your company real advantages like higher customer happiness, lower customer turnover, and higher income.

6. Make learning opportunities available

Although creating a customer-focused culture is a process that takes time, using these tactics will put you on the right track.

Keep staff members informed of developments, solicit their opinions and suggestions, and provide them access to tools like Salesforce Trailhead training courses to aid in the development of customer-focused competencies. Options abound, such as teaching customer support representatives the fundamentals of customer journeys and honing their communication abilities. In the end, organizations establish a compelling offer for consumers and a sizable competitive advantage by cultivating a culture where customers' demands are at the center of every encounter. However, there is still another reason why companies should prioritize their customers.

Industries as a whole are being disrupted by technology at an unprecedented rate. Recognize your customer's demands to foresee or even create disruption. History has repeatedly demonstrated that it is better to cause trouble for yourself than to stand by and let someone else do it to you. Ask Blockbuster, please.

How to strengthen your customer focus approach

An efficient customer-focus strategy must be developed on both an operational and an emotional level. You may establish genuine, open, and transparent relationships with your consumers by implementing a solid customer focus approach. It also directs you in putting the proper systems and procedures in place. Here are six suggestions to help you stay focused on relationship management and process improvement:

1. Promote cooperation

Teams must collaborate to produce a consistent, superior experience if they are to transform into a customer-focused business. In reality, customers want businesses to work together on their behalf more than 70% of the time.

Sales and support teams may work together to:

When a consumer expresses interest in learning more about a new product, an agent can alert sales. Alternatively, a sales representative might divert a more technical query to an agent with expertise in that field.

And working together pays dividends. According to Benchmark research, sales and support teams who work together generate more leads, develop more prospects, and win more transactions.

However, cooperation shouldn't interfere with your team's ability to work quickly because doing so simply serves to frustrate the client. A connective layer of tissue that combines client data across departments is therefore necessary for efficient customer collaboration. This enables teams to exchange ideas without

1. Interrupting their workflow

2. Making the consumer aware of what's happening in the background

3. Encourage your clients to feel heard

Every consumer has a backstory. Customers, however, do not like to be required to retell that tale each time they connect with your brand. Additionally, clients won't likely recall your business as being customer-focused if they feel neglected because they need to repeat themselves. Making the consumer feel heard, according to Brummel, is a big aspect of customer attention. And the encounter may rapidly turn negative if they don't feel heard.

Imagine having to reintroduce yourself to a coworker and bring up your previous conversation every time you pass them in the workplace kitchen. Although it is neither personal nor customer-focused, this is frequently how organizations interact with their clients.

Businesses need the same connecting connection to make sure that happy consumers feel heard. This offers them complete information on the customer, including

a. Name;

b. Account details; and

c. When they last communicated with them.

Teams will then have access to the pertinent context and conversation history they require to provide clients with the individualized experiences they deserve.

3. Go where your consumers are.

It can seem simpler to concentrate on one form of communication and deliver an excellent experience there. However, according to data from Zendesk, interacting via your clients' preferred channels is a significant loyalty-boosting strategy.

The data is unambiguous: An effortless customer experience is the best. Customers shouldn't have to exert any effort to find your brand; they don't want to. Because of this, customer-focused businesses meet their clients where they are. Customers are now able to get in touch whenever and however they choose.

It might be eye-opening to evaluate your customer base's demographics and the kinds of queries you receive most frequently. Industry standards may advise you to provide a certain channel. However, you could discover that a sizable portion of your clients want a mobile-first solution. Because your consumers are on mobile devices, you can think about integrating WhatsApp, SMS, or another mobile messaging platform.

Again, linking discussions across channels will be largely dependent on the 360-degree perspective of the consumer. It guarantees that context follows the customer. This enables your company to respond promptly and personally to all inquiries, regardless of when or how they are made.

4. Use criticism to improve

Another crucial element in developing a customer-focused business is understanding how to manage client feedback. Customer-focused businesses do not treat customer complaints like a game of dodgeball.

Amplification of the customer's voice and use of their comments to improve the experience

This might incorporate:

a. Sending surveys to your customers

b. Starting an online forum where users may discuss your goods or services and vote for new feature requests.

It's crucial to establish a feedback loop with your clients. Like any healthy connection, your relationship with them should be mutually beneficial.

One of the first stages in developing a customer-focused culture is to see customers as collaborators and partners rather than as mere consumers of your goods, according to Brummel.

5. Integrate data and empathy

Companies no longer need to assume what their consumers want or make decisions for them due to the growing amount of data accessible. They might instead focus on the current trends.

However, using data in a customer-focused manner doesn't entail doing it carelessly. Instead, it entails fusing empathy with facts. This entails a. Giving data context; b. Applying data empathetically, and c.

Using data to improve customer intimacy—gaining knowledge of the people using your product and their needs.

To make sure a change is relevant to the individuals it affects, your product team can, for example, link a product update with customer support data. Or, a marketing team might: a.Adjust content based on where each client is in the customer journey rather than sending each customer an identical email.

b. Group material based on prior emails a consumer has opened.

However, segregated data frequently stops businesses from utilizing it aggressively and in a manner that serves the client. That's because they lack the necessary context. To properly manage and evaluate your data, you'll need to link insights across systems and applications.

6. Apply AI to anticipate client wants.

Businesses that put their clients first don't only respond to their needs; they also go above and beyond to satisfy them. Additionally, proactive experiences don't have to be difficult or expensive thanks to AI. To proactively lower customer complaints, support employees may, for instance, utilize machine learning to forecast customer happiness. Alternatively, sales teams may use a chatbot to proactively greet clients before they leave their shopping cart or demo request form because of unanswered queries.

7. Encourage the groups that assist consumers.

The direct interactions your customer service personnel have with your consumers affect how they feel about your brand. When an agent is unhappy or overworked, customers can tell, and it can ruin their experience. Unfortunately, customer service positions carry a substantial risk of burnout. To enable agents to effectively do their responsibilities, businesses must assist their support staff.

For instance, just 1 in 5 agents say they are very satisfied with the quality of the training they have access to, and 62 percent say that receiving additional skills-based training would help them perform better.

Chapter 4

Reaching new heights in your business

How to Launch and Expand Your Business

Your company has reached a stage where things are steady. You have a strong team in place, you generate steady revenue, and you're prepared to advance your business. But what does the following level entail? How do you get there, too?

There is no one-size-fits-all response to these queries, but there are certain overarching guidelines you can stick to effectively launch and expand your firm.

1. Define Your Goals First

Take a step back and outline your goals for your business as your first step. What are your long-range objectives? What are your main concerns? What can you do shortly?

By providing clear answers to these inquiries, you may create a clear action plan for the future.

2. Pay Attention to Your Core Competencies

You must concentrate on your core strengths if you want to expand your company. These are the areas where you shine and where your clients receive the greatest benefit.

You'll be able to more effectively utilize your resources and get a competitive edge by concentrating on your core strengths. This will become increasingly important as you expand your business.

3. Create A Powerful Team

You'll need to develop a solid team to back you as your company expands. People with the knowledge and expertise required to support you in reaching your objectives should be a part of this team.

Build a staff that is committed to the same goals as you do for the company. This will make it easier to make sure that everyone is pursuing the same goals.

4. Spend Money On Marketing

Any company that wants to expand must invest in marketing. You may expand your client and market base as well as develop your brand's recognition and authority through marketing. You may experiment with several marketing channels, so it's critical to identify the ones that are most effective for your company. To assist you in creating and putting into practice an efficient marketing plan, you might also think about employing a marketing consultancy or agency.

5. Concentrate On Retaining Customers

Along with attracting new clients, it's crucial to concentrate on keeping your current clientele. The best approach to do this is to deliver top-notch customer service and foster a happy client journey.

Additionally, you want to think about introducing loyalty plans and other retention techniques. Even if you expand your business, these might help you retain your clients coming back.

6. A Growth Plan

You'll need to make sure that your operations can scale as your company expands. To support a larger firm, the appropriate systems and procedures must be in place.

A financial strategy should be in place as well. By doing this, you'll be sure to have the resources required to support your development.

7. Remain adaptable

Finally, it's critical to maintain flexibility as your firm expands. As your company grows, things will inevitably change, so be ready to modify your strategies as necessary.

You may effectively launch and expand your business by adhering to these suggestions. Just keep in mind that there isn't a one-size-fits-all answer;

because every organization is different, you'll need to customize your strategy.

The Best Advice for Launching a Business

You are eager to launch your fantastic company concept. However, there are a few steps you should take before starting your firm if you want to position yourself for success. The following is the best company startup advice:

1. Research the topic.

It's crucial to investigate and comprehend the market you're entering before starting your firm. What patterns are there? Who may be your future clients? What are your rivals up to? You may build a solid foundation for your company by providing answers to these questions.

2.Create a business plan, second.

You may use it to create objectives, monitor your advancement, and make crucial choices as you go.

Don't neglect this stage; doing so will boost the likelihood of your company's success.

3. Select the appropriate legal framework.

You have a variety of legal structures from which to pick for your company, and your decision will have an impact on matters of taxation, responsibility, and other law. To safeguard your assets and yourself, it's crucial to pick the appropriate legal structure for your company.

4. Organize Yourself.

It's time to get organized once you've launched your company concept. This covers all aspects, from establishing an accounting system to developing policies for responding to consumer inquiries. You can manage your business more successfully and efficiently if you get organized.

5. Choose The Proper Location.

You must pick a site that is handy for your consumers if you plan to offer goods or services there. You must pick a domain name and web hosting provider if you're beginning an internet business. In either case, be sure to give your choice of site some thought so that you can draw in the correct clients.

6. Market Your Company.

It's time to begin marketing your firm now that it is operational. This might involve doing anything from building a website to distributing business cards to taking part in neighborhood events. Spreading the word about your organization is crucial for bringing in clients and expanding your enterprise.

Although starting a business is a major task, it may be rewarding on both a personal and professional level. You can achieve achievement by paying attention to these suggestions.

The Different Business Types

There are several distinct business models, and each has certain advantages and disadvantages. An essential first step in beginning your own business is choosing the industry that best fits your skills and interests.

A single proprietorship is the most basic and uncomplicated type of business. You are the only owner and decision-maker for the business. Since you and the firm are legally one and the same, you are liable for all of the debts and obligations of the business. Small businesses frequently choose sole proprietorships because they are easy to start up and reasonably priced.

A business with at least two proprietors is called a partnership. All partnerships have two things in common: everyone participates equally in decision-making, and everyone is personally responsible for the debts and liabilities of the business. Partnerships can exist in a wide variety of ways. Although forming partnerships can be a great way to pool resources and talents, doing so can be challenging due to the likelihood of partner disputes.

Corporation: A corporation is a type of business that is separate from its owners legally. Corporations are desirable to businesses for a number of reasons, including their perpetual existence, the owners' restricted liability, and the ability to raise funds by selling shares. Compared to other company forms, corporations can be more expensive to start and maintain, and they are also subject to more stringent regulations.

The traits of a corporation and a partnership are combined to form a limited liability company (LLC). LLCs have the limited liability protection of a corporation but are taxed like partnerships. Because LLCs are so easy to establish up and manage, they are a popular choice for small enterprises.

No matter what kind of business you decide to create, there are a few essential steps you must do. Choosing a legal structure for your business, obtaining the necessary permits and licenses, and registering your business with the government are some of these steps.

These steps should be finished before you start writing your business strategy. Your business plan will outline your goals and provide a roadmap for achieving them.

It's important to remember that starting a business needs perseverance, hard work, and patience. With work and dedication, though, you could succeed in your endeavor to launch your own firm.

The Advantages of Opening a Business

Having your own business may be incredibly satisfying and has numerous benefits. some of the advantages of starting your own business are:

1. You have control: As the boss, you have the last say in all matters. You have the power to determine the course of your own life and the course of your company.

2. You can be creative: When you own your own company, you have complete creative freedom. You don't need anyone else's permission to come up with fresh ideas and put them into practice.

3. You have complete control over your schedule: One of the benefits of being your boss is having complete control over your schedule. You are free to work in the early morning or late at night. People who have families or other obligations throughout the typical workday may find this to be quite beneficial.

4. You can earn more money: If you succeed, you can earn significantly more money than you would if you were working for someone else. Additionally, if you want to sell your company someday, you'll have the opportunity to earn even more money.

5. The most alluring feature of establishing your own business is certainly the fact that you get to be your boss. No one else has to answer you; you get to make the decisions.

These are only a few of the numerous advantages of starting your own company. If you're considering establishing your own business, thoroughly consider the advantages and disadvantages to determine if it's the best choice for you.

How to Affordably Launch a Business

You've got a terrific company concept. You have a strong commitment to your good or service and are prepared to expand your company. However, you must first acquire enough funds to begin generating money.

There are several methods to fund your business, and the ideal one for you will depend on your particular situation. Consider the following choices:

1. Individual savings. You can fund your business using any savings you may have. For those with a low-risk company concept and little startup capital, this is frequently the ideal alternative.

2. Family and friends. You may also enlist the financial support of your friends and family to finance your business. If you have a strong business strategy and are confident in your ability to succeed, this can be an excellent choice. Just be sure you invest this money rather than using it as a loan, and be ready to pay interest on it.

3. Investors in angels. Wealthy individuals who invest in fast-growing companies are known as angel investors. If you can locate an angel investor who supports your company concept, they will be able to provide you with the money you need to launch.

4. Entrepreneurs in the capital. Professional investors known as venture capitalists make investments in fast-growing companies. Compared

to angel investors, they frequently invest bigger quantities of money, but they also anticipate greater returns.

5. Credit cards. Additionally, you might seek a bank loan to finance your company. For companies with assets to give as security for the loan, such as property or equipment, this is frequently a desirable alternative.

6. Governmental funding. You can qualify for government funds if your company is involved in research and development to help finance it.

7. Equity-based lending. When you raise money by selling a piece of your company, this is called equity financing. If you don't want to take on debt or cede management of your business, this may be a viable choice. It's crucial to keep in mind, though, that equity investors will demand a return on their investment, so be ready to part up some of your earnings.

Whatever you do, make sure to conduct your homework and consult experts before making any judgments.

You'll be well on your way to expanding your company after you've secured the initial funding you require.

Creating a profitable business

Do you want to grow your business to a new level as an entrepreneur? If so, you should concentrate on creating a prosperous business. This may be done by laying a solid foundation, coming up with a winning plan, and putting together the ideal team.

Any business needs a solid foundation, but a fast-growing firm needs it more than any other. Your company should be built on a strong business model, a defined goal and vision, and the essential infrastructure. Your company will be more likely to collapse when faced with obstacles if it doesn't have a solid basis.

Creating a winning plan is yet another essential component of creating a successful business. Your plan should be created to assist you in achieving your objectives and aims. It must be founded on a deep comprehension of both your target market and your industry's competitors. Your plan should also be adaptable enough to adjust and develop with your company.

Finally, without the correct people in place, no business can succeed. Any company's success depends on putting together a team of talented and motivated employees. Your team should be comprised of individuals who are dedicated to your goal and vision and who have complementary talents and experiences.

Building a solid foundation, creating a successful plan, and putting together the proper staff are the three essential areas you should concentrate on if you want to take your company to the next level.

Managing Your Business in a Technological Age

The way businesses operate has completely altered because of the internet. The ability to launch a business has never been simpler, and there are more ways than ever to connect with people across the world. But there is more competition as a result of this enhanced accessibility. You must be able to properly run your business in the age of technology if you want to flourish in the market today.

How to Run a Business in the Digital Age

Due to the Internet, company operations have undergone a significant change. There are more methods than ever to interact with people across the world, and starting a business has never been easier. But because of this improved accessibility, there is greater competition. If you want to succeed in the market today, you must be able to manage your company effectively in the era of technology.

You need to make sure that your use of social media is efficient in addition to having a solid website. This is a fantastic approach to engage with and establish a connection with your target audience. It's also an excellent strategy to monitor your competitors and remain informed about developments in your business.

In the age of technology, there are a lot of additional tasks you must complete to operate your company successfully. For instance, you should ensure that your data is protected and backed up and that you have a disaster recovery strategy in place just in case.

To make the most of the newest technology, you must also spend in training for yourself and your team as well as maintain your software and systems up to date.

Make sure you're ready for the obstacles of running a business in the current day if you're serious about pushing it to the next level. You may get an advantage over the competition and position yourself for success by paying attention to the advice given above.

From Small Fish to Big Fish Guidelines for Making Your Idea a Reality

1. Specify Your Concept.

What plans does your company have? What services or goods will you provide? Which issue will you resolve? Be as detailed as you can.

2. Research the topic.

Verify that there is a market for what you are selling. Ask prospective consumers for their opinions. Do some competitor research.

3. Make a business plan.

This serves as a corporate road map. It will support your concept development, goal-setting, and progress monitoring.

4. Select the Proper Location.

You must locate a suitable area if you're beginning a brick-and-mortar firm. Take into account elements such as foot traffic, parking, and public transportation.

5. Create A Strong Team.

Assemble a team of individuals who will support your endeavor and has the knowledge and abilities necessary to make it successful.

6. Raise Money.

To start your business, you will need money. Find investors or submit a loan application.

7. Promote your company.

Spread the word about your company. To reach your target audience, use public relations, advertising, and social media.

8. Track Your Development.

Monitor your revenue and spending. To make sure you're on pace to achieve your goals, adjust your plan as necessary. You can raise your chances of success by paying attention to these suggestions.

What Characteristics Characterize Successful Businesses?

A successful business has several essential components, but some are more crucial than others. The most crucial components of a prosperous company are:

1. A succinct and clear business strategy: A successful business requires a well-written business plan. It describes your company's objectives, strategies, and plans for achieving them. It will be challenging to make your business effective without a defined plan.

2. A potent marketing plan: One of the most crucial components of every organization is its marketing plan. It will be tough to produce sales and expand your firm without a solid marketing plan.

3. A committed team: A successful company needs a group of committed workers who are enthusiastic

about what they do. It will be tough to succeed without a solid team.

4. Financial stability: To expand and prosper, a firm must be financially stable. A successful business will be challenging to maintain without financial security.

5. A good reputation: Any successful firm must have a good reputation. It will be tough to draw consumers and expand your firm without a solid reputation.

These are only a handful of the essential components of a prosperous company. If you can keep your attention on these factors, you will be well on your way to growing your company.

Conclusion

Asking questions and listening are two of the most crucial components of selling. The prospect will give you all you need to know to close the sale if you ask the right questions. Effective listening techniques will give you the strength and self-control to ascertain facts and requirements before formulating a response that prompts the customer to make a choice. That seems so easy, man.

Why then do none of them purchase when you try to sell them? Because…

The questions you're posing are not being answered well. You're not paying attention to what the prospect has to say. You prejudge the prospect's personality, anticipate their responses, and cut the conversation because of your prior notions about them. You disregard asking questions and paying attention to what is being said because you believe you already know the answers. You have not ascertained the prospect's actual demands. If you don't know what your needs are, how can you meet them?

Q.Are you asking prospective customers questions that encourage them to express their accomplishments? These are rapport-building questions as well as sales ones.

Q. Does the prospect answer the query that they haven't considered before? You appear different, better, and at the top of your game when you use new twists.

Q. Does the question offer a conclusive response that brings the presenting process to a close? When you use terms like "don't you," "isn't it," "shouldn't you," and "doesn't it," you're giving the prospect the option to accept a certain portion of your presentation and go on to the next one.

Q. Does the query directly address the prospect's (commercial) circumstance? You are more likely to receive a direct response if your query is direct.

Q.Does the query directly address the goals of the prospect? Are you asking questions that the potential customer can relate to? areas where the prospect is forced to provide honest responses.

Q. Does the query elicit information from the potential customer that makes the sale process simpler? How will your product or service be used? What are their expectations?

Q. Does the query foster a favorable environment that will enable a sale to be made? Is the query provoking or provocative? When you ask a prospect a question, make him ponder rather than make him angry.

Q. Are you returning questions when a potential customer asks you one? Prospect: Is delivery possible in two weeks? Is that when you need it delivered, salesperson?

Q.Do you have any last queries? a query the resolution of which validates the sale. Do you have 10 or 12 distinct closing questions prepared that you may practice and utilize as needed? You probably do not.

Do you wish to learn this science? For each of the aforementioned twelve problems, come up with two or three questions that you may use in your selling process. I'll offer you two promises if you do.

1. It will be quite challenging.

2. You will become a better, more lucrative salesperson as a result of doing it.

As breathing is to life, questions are to sales. You will perish if you don't ask them. If you answer them poorly, you won't die right away, but it will happen eventually.

The right question will result in a sale as the response.

What is the most crucial ability a salesperson has to possess?

Between a sale and a lack of a sale is where the significance of asking properly resides.